Contents

Dog

Follow these steps to draw.

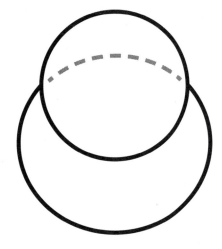

© Chalkboard Publishing

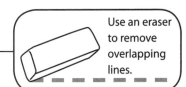

Use an eraser to remove overlapping lines.

Cat

Follow these steps to draw.

1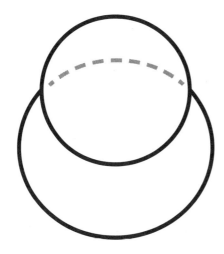

2

3

4

Use an eraser to remove overlapping lines.

Frog

Follow these steps to draw.

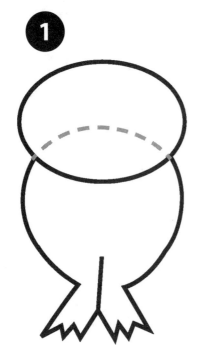

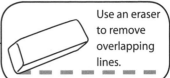

Use an eraser to remove overlapping lines.

Mouse

Follow these steps to draw.

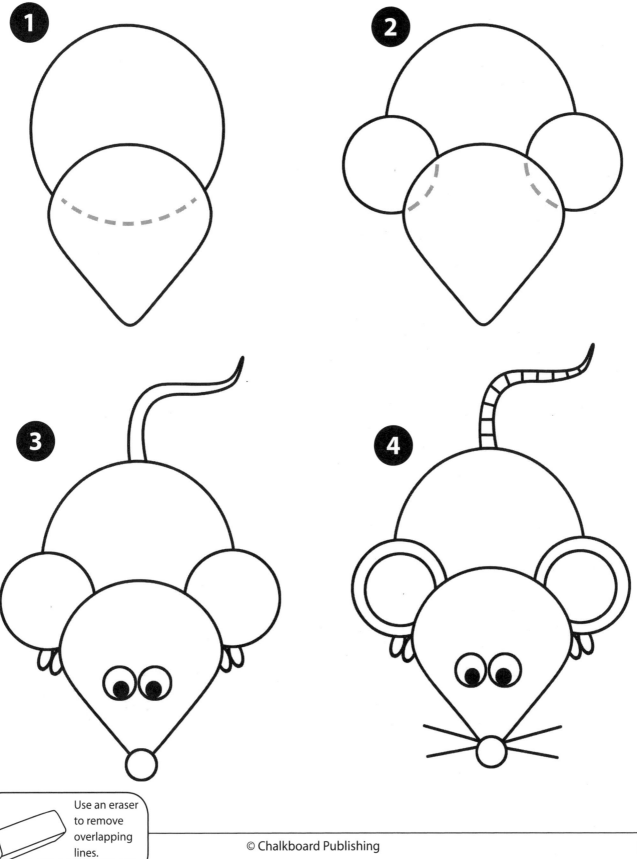

Use an eraser to remove overlapping lines.

Turtle

Follow these steps to draw.

Pets Writing Prompts

- If my pet could talk…
- My pet _____ is special because…
- I would like a great big _____ for a pet because…
- I love my pet _____ because…
- If I had a pet store…
- One day, I let my pet mouse loose in the house.
- Each day, my pet mouse grew bigger and bigger…
- My pet cat likes to bark like a dog.
- My cat has a special talent…
- My cat gets attention by…
- My dog saved the day when…
- My dog can do some amazing tricks.
- Dogs are like people because…
- My pet turtle is a champion…
- Write about how to take care of a pet.
- Tell about where your pet lives, what it eats, and how it spends its time.
- Describe a typical day in a life of a pet.
- Write a letter to convince your parents to adopt a pet _____.
- Write about how a turtle protects itself.

Chicken

Follow these steps to draw.

Cow

Follow these steps to draw.

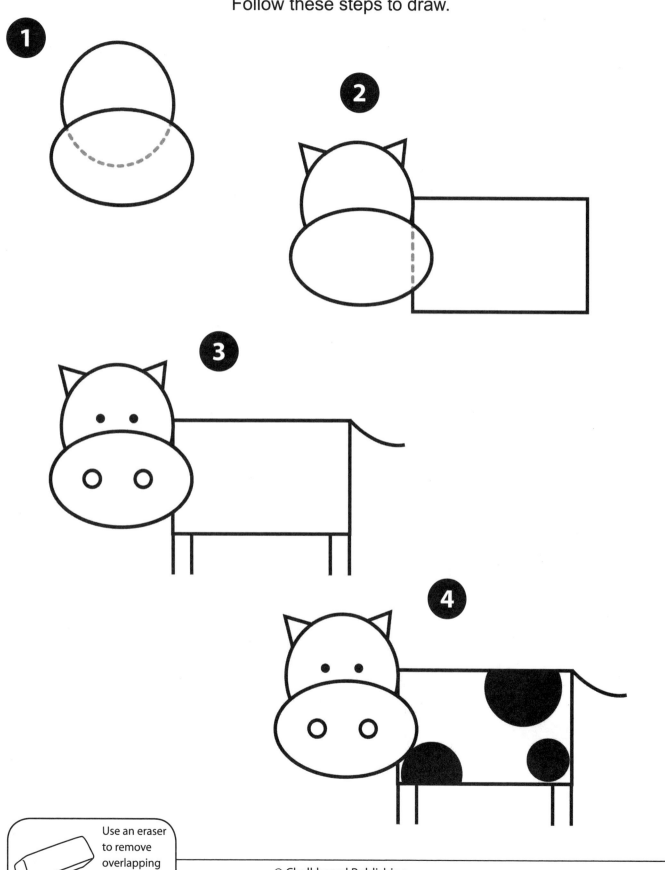

Use an eraser to remove overlapping lines.

Goat

Follow these steps to draw.

Use an eraser to remove overlapping lines.

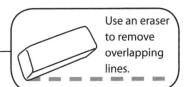

Pig

Follow these steps to draw.

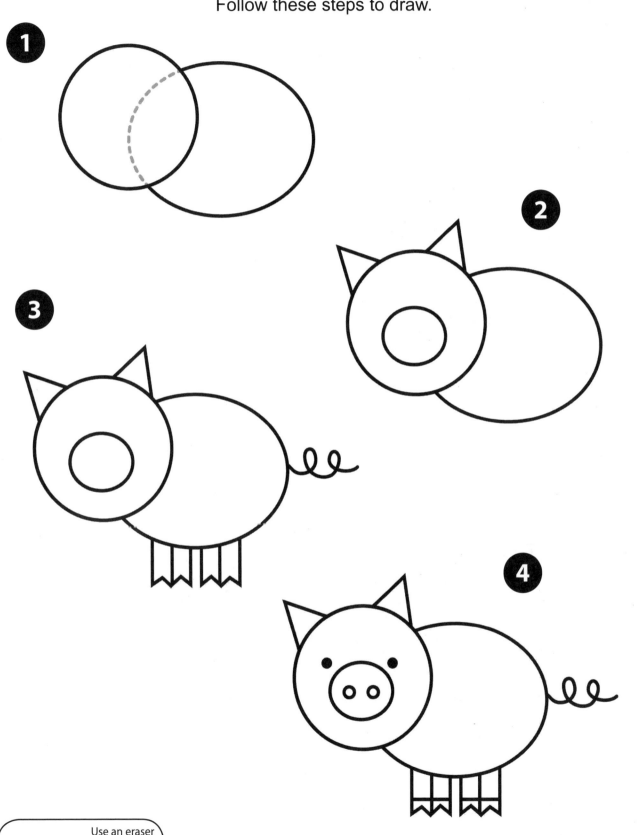

1

2

3

4

Use an eraser to remove overlapping lines.

Rabbit

Follow these steps to draw.

© Chalkboard Publishing

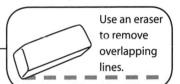

Use an eraser to remove overlapping lines.

Sheep

Follow these steps to draw.

Farm Animals Writing Prompts

- ◆ It was a sunny spring morning on the farm, when all of a sudden…

- ◆ Everyone on the farm was excited for the baby chicks to hatch…

- ◆ The mother hen was very protective of her chicks.

- ◆ The little chicks loved to hide.

- ◆ The cow ate grass in the field. She said "moo" when she bumped into a…

- ◆ There was once a brown cow that made chocolate milk.

- ◆ Once upon a time, there was a goat who lived on the top of a big hill.

- ◆ One day, a goat climbed a mountain. When he reached the top, he saw…

- ◆ The little pigs loved to play in the mud!

- ◆ The pig was very hungry. When he got back to the barn, he saw his favorite dinner. It was…

- ◆ Mother rabbit heard a noise by the bushes. A moment later, baby rabbit…

- ◆ The rabbits were exploring the vegetable garden, when they discovered…

- ◆ The sheep loved to dance.

- ◆ Sheila the sheep wished her wool was the color of the rainbow…

- ◆ In the big red barn, there lived…

- ◆ It was a strange day when the farmer discovered the animals could talk!

- ◆ A typical day at the farm starts off with…

Bee

Follow these steps to draw.

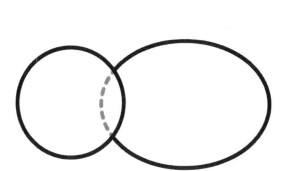

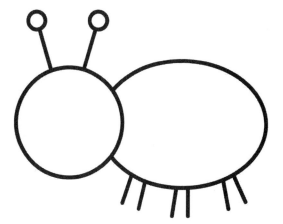

Use an eraser to remove overlapping lines.

Caterpillar

Follow these steps to draw.

1

2

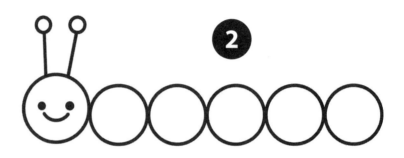

3

4

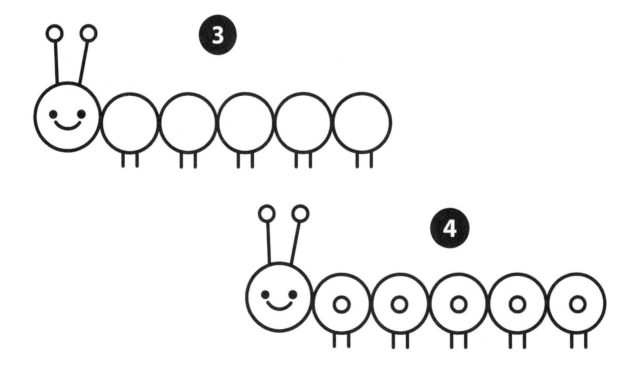

Butterfly

Follow these steps to draw.

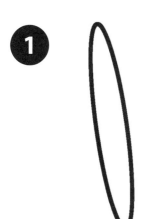

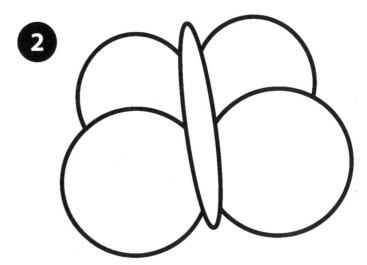

Firefly

Follow these steps to draw.

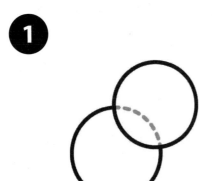

Use an eraser to remove overlapping lines.

Ladybug

Follow these steps to draw.

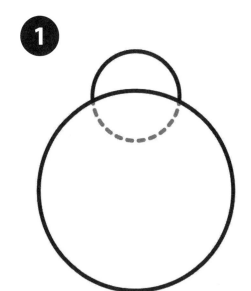

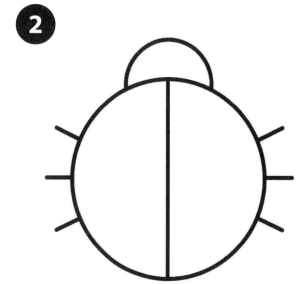

Use an eraser to remove overlapping lines.

Snail

Follow these steps to draw.

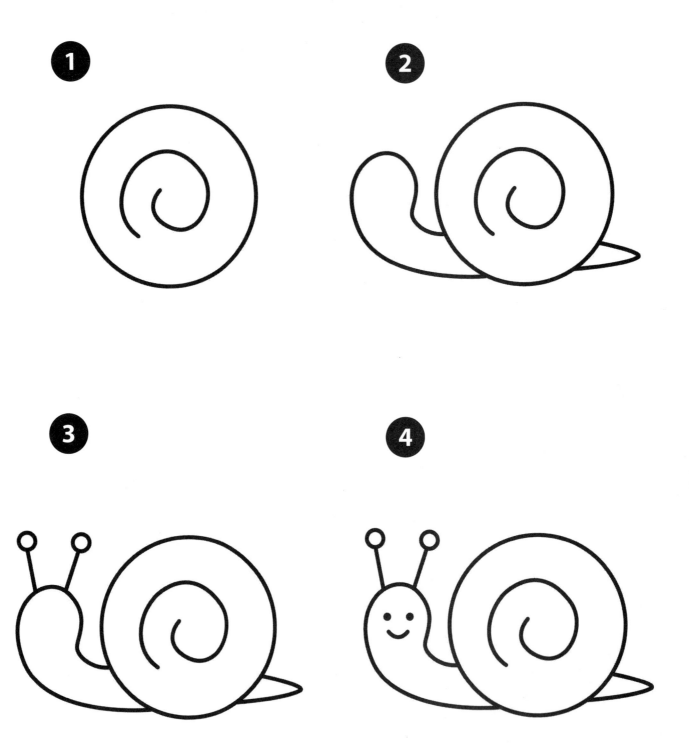

© Chalkboard Publishing

Spider

Follow these steps to draw.

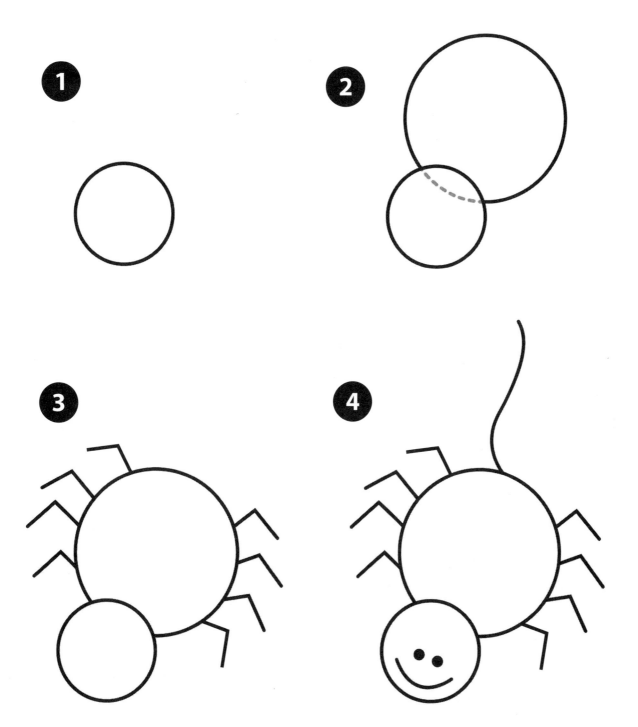

Use an eraser to remove overlapping lines.

Garden Creatures Writing Prompts

◆ The bee buzzed around the hive. It was an exciting day…

◆ The bee saw a flower in the distance. She flew over to it and discovered an amazing…

◆ The caterpillar crawled up a tree. When she got there, it was very sunny so she…

◆ The fuzzy caterpillar looked all around to find somewhere to make his cocoon. When he looked up he saw the perfect branch. He crawled up the tree, then…

◆ The butterfly thought she was very beautiful.

◆ Describe the life cycle of a butterfly.

◆ One night, as the firefly flew through the forest, he saw a little boy. The little boy…

◆ Make up a tale about how fireflies got their glow.

◆ The ladybugs crawled closer to the picnic blanket, then…

◆ How did the ladybug get it spots?

◆ This was no ordinary snail…

◆ The snail crawled through the grass toward a leaf, then…

◆ One day, while a spider was spinning her web, she noticed a raindrop. She crawled over to it, then…

◆ The schoolyard was full of spiders.

◆ Describe the typical day of your favorite insect.

◆ Write a friendly letter to an insect.

◆ List five interview questions for your favorite insect.

Elephant

Follow these steps to draw.

1

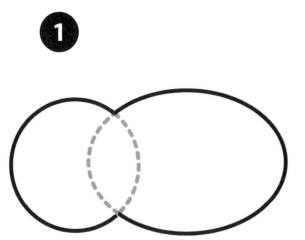

2

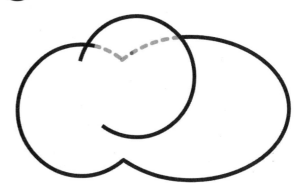

3

4

Use an eraser to remove overlapping lines.

Giraffe

Follow these steps to draw.

1

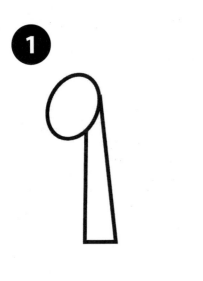

2

3

4

Use an eraser to remove overlapping lines.

Lion

Follow these steps to draw.

1

2

3

4

Use an eraser to remove overlapping lines.

Tiger

Follow these steps to draw.

1

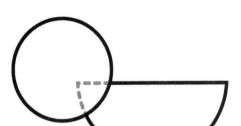

2

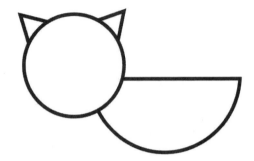

3

4

© Chalkboard Publishing

Use an eraser to remove overlapping lines.

Parrot

Follow these steps to draw.

1

2

3

4

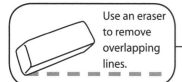

Snake

Follow these steps to draw.

1

2

3

4

Zoo Animals Writing Prompts

◆ The baby elephants played happily in the water. They splashed and played until…

◆ The elephant family were taking a walk, when all of a sudden…

◆ The giraffe and his friend walked around looking for a snack. They saw a tall tree, so they…

◆ A giraffe has a very long neck because…

◆ Lionel the lion had a problem. He lost his roar!

◆ The playful lion cubs were exploring their home at the zoo, when they noticed an open door…

◆ The parrot flew from tree to tree in the rainforest, when she noticed the sun starting to set. She began to fly home, when…

◆ I took my pet parrot to school…

◆ Sam the snake liked to slither around and sneak up on his friends.

◆ Snakes are interesting, but they are also a little scary.

◆ The tiger was excited to go on adventure.

◆ The little tiger was told to be good, but…

◆ The animals at the zoo decided to sneak out one night.

◆ A _____ escaped from the zoo.

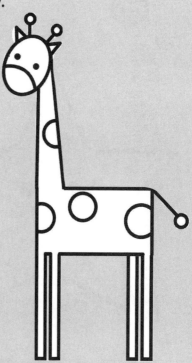

Sea Star

Follow these steps to draw.

1

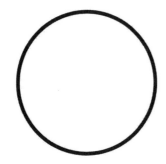

2

3

4

Use an eraser to remove overlapping lines.

Crab

Follow these steps to draw.

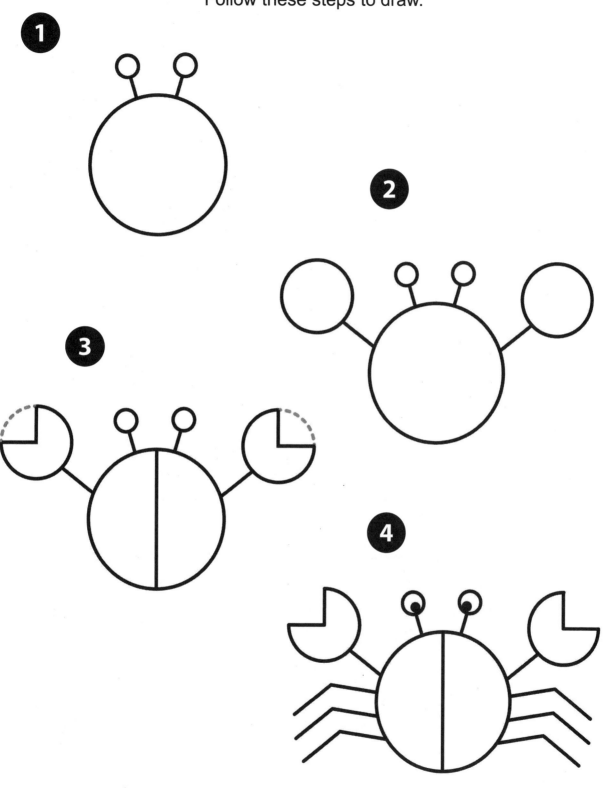

Jellyfish

Follow these steps to draw.

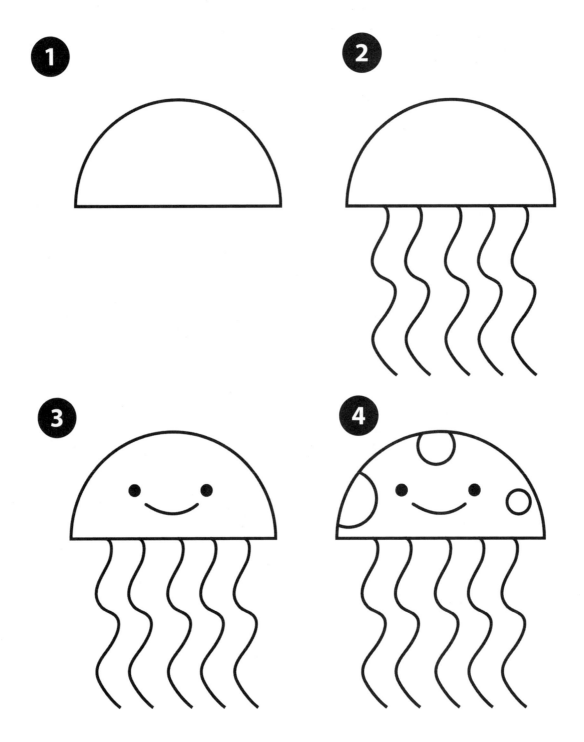

Octopus

Follow these steps to draw.

Use an eraser to remove overlapping lines.

Dolphin

Follow these steps to draw.

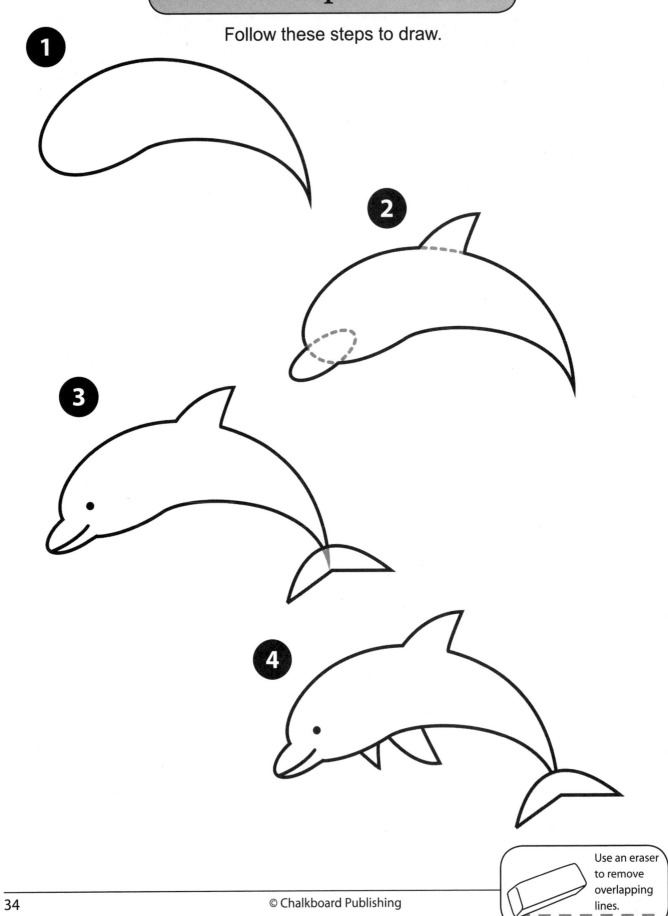

© Chalkboard Publishing

Use an eraser to remove overlapping lines.

Fish

Follow these steps to draw.

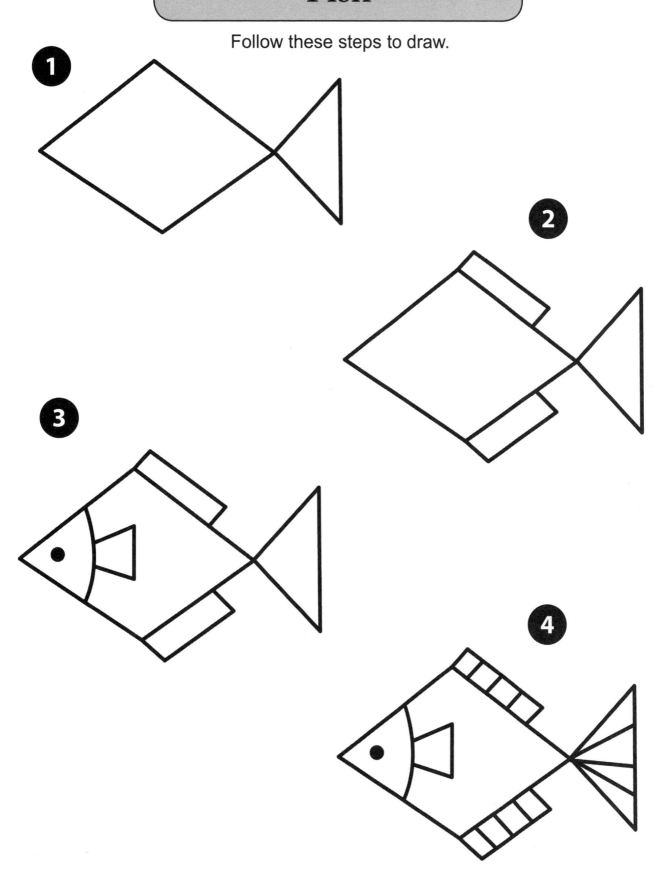

Shark

Follow these steps to draw.

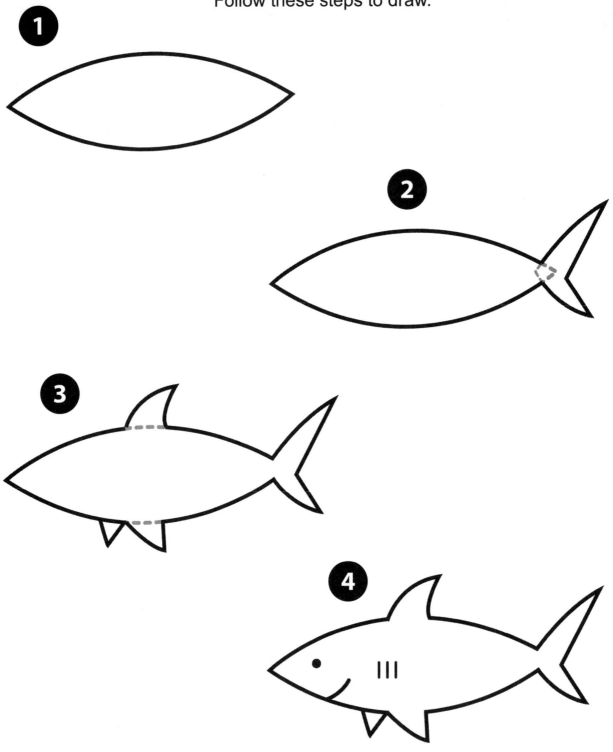

© Chalkboard Publishing

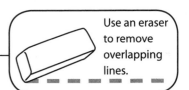

Use an eraser to remove overlapping lines.

Swordfish

Follow these steps to draw.

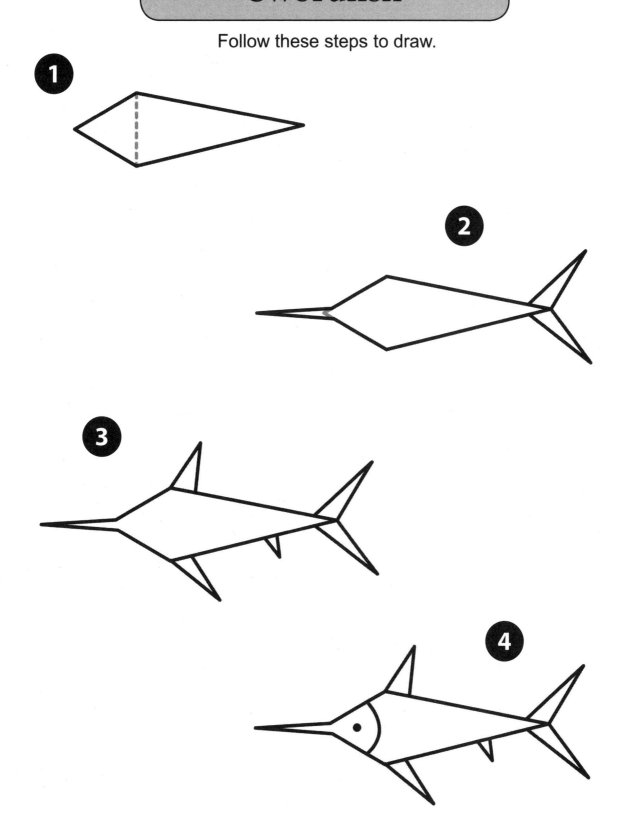

Use an eraser to remove overlapping lines.

Whale

Follow these steps to draw.

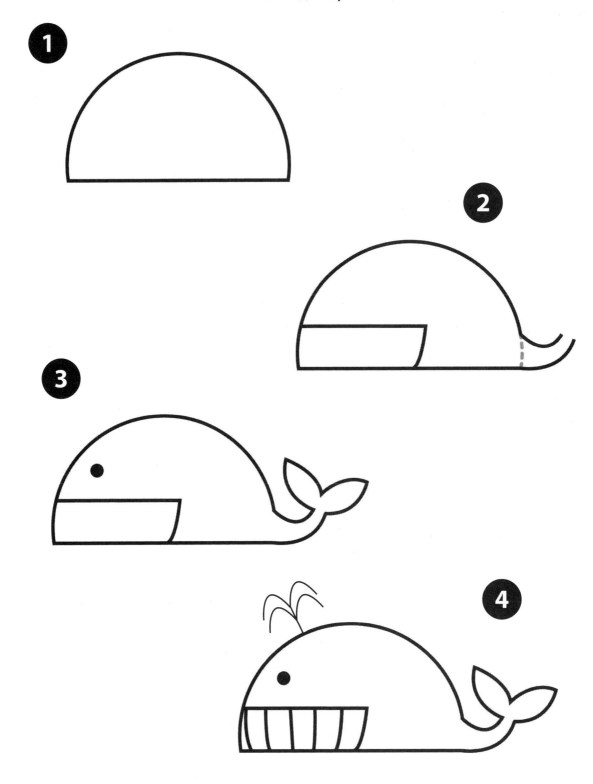

© Chalkboard Publishing

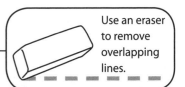

Use an eraser to remove overlapping lines.

Underwater Creatures Writing Prompts

◆ One day, a little crab went for a swim. When he got out of the ocean, he walked across the beach. Then…

◆ The crab snapped his claws as he scuttled along the beach.

◆ The dolphins swam together through the ocean. In the distance, they saw a boat.

◆ The playful dolphin saw a family swimming in the ocean. She swam up to them, then…

◆ Daisy the fish woke up one morning and looked outside her tank. She usually saw more fish when she looked out, but today she saw…

◆ The fish swam closer to the surface of the water. They saw something big and shiny in the distance. It was…

◆ The school of fish raced to find the…

◆ The octopus reached for the coral reef with one of her tentacles. She grabbed it, then…

◆ The jellyfish bobbed through the ocean enjoying a snack when her mom called her to come back home. When she got home, she…

◆ The children at the aquarium said "wow" when they saw the jellyfish change colors. The jellyfish was…

◆ The shark chased a fish that it wanted to eat for dinner, but then…

◆ The sea star family nibbled at some delicious coral reef when all of a sudden there was a knock on the other side of the reef. They looked up and saw…

◆ The sea star and her twin sister floated lazily through the sea when they noticed…

◆ The swordfish raced quickly to catch up to his friends. When he reached them, they decided to…

◆ The people watched as the whale spit water from its blow hole. The whale was so close to the people that…

◆ My underwater adventure began when…

Cactus

Follow these steps to draw.

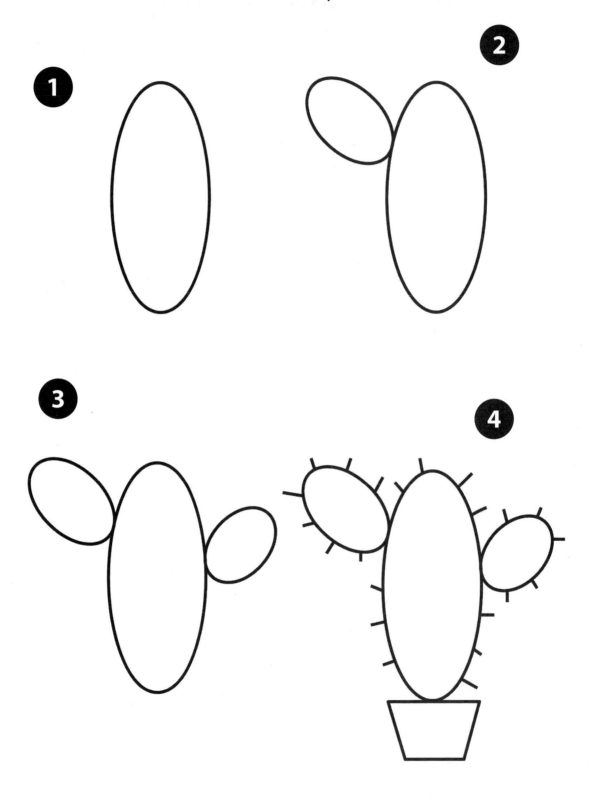

© Chalkboard Publishing

Willow Tree

Follow these steps to draw.

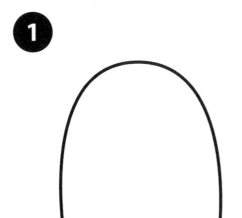

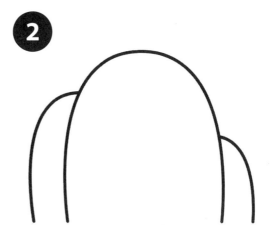

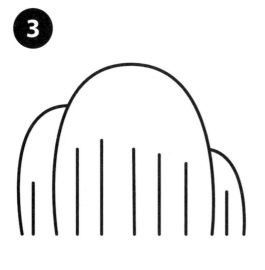

Palm Tree

Follow these steps to draw.

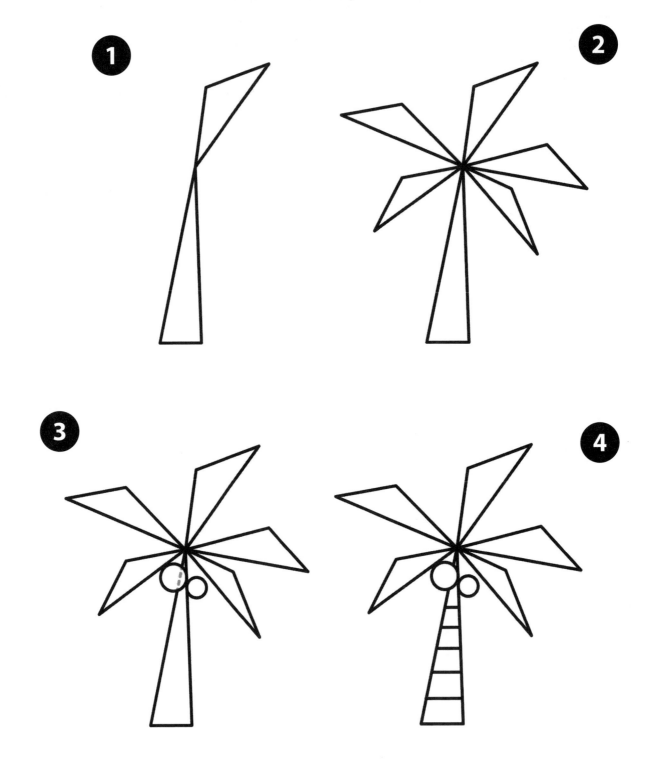

© Chalkboard Publishing

Use an eraser to remove overlapping lines.

Pine Tree

Follow these steps to draw.

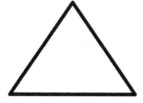

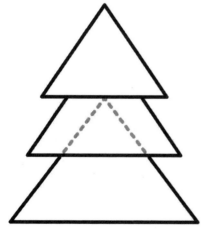

Use an eraser to remove overlapping lines.

Tree

Follow these steps to draw.

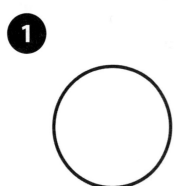

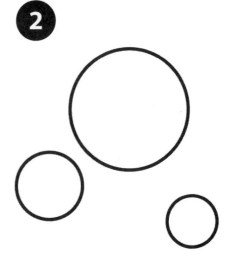

Rosebush

Follow these steps to draw.

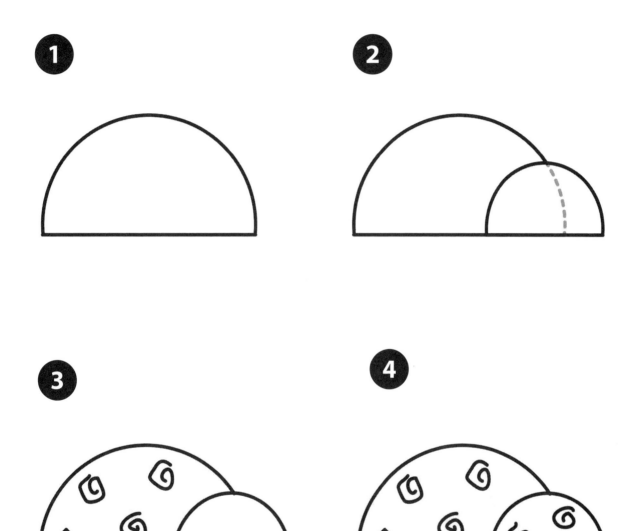

1

2

3

4

Use an eraser to remove overlapping lines.

Rose

Follow these steps to draw.

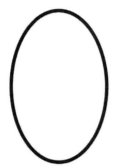

Mushroom

Follow these steps to draw.

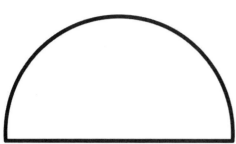

Carnation

Follow these steps to draw.

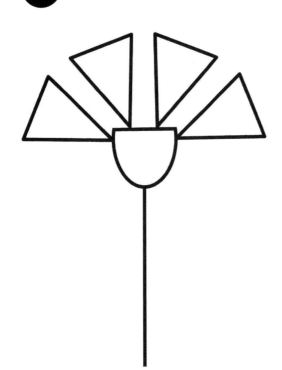

Flower

Follow these steps to draw.

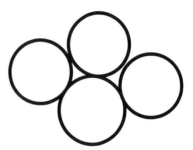

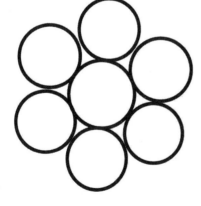

Tulip

Follow these steps to draw.

1

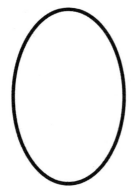

2

3

4

Use an eraser to remove overlapping lines.

Trees and Plants Writing Prompts

◆ This was a very special flower. It bloomed even in the winter!

◆ The girl sat on a hill as she sniffed a beautiful bouquet of flowers. The flowers were…

◆ The rosebush grew the most beautiful roses. The roses were magic!

◆ The tulips in the garden were in full bloom. The children watched as the wind blew the petals back and forth. The next day…

◆ Deep inside an enchanted forest there was a giant mushroom…

◆ I had never seen a palm tree before…

◆ At the top of the palm tree there was a…

◆ The pine tree was home to…

◆ This was the perfect tree for…

◆ This was a magical tree that grew…

◆ The children planted tulip bulbs in the garden. When spring arrived…

◆ The giant willow tree provided shade and shelter for all the animals in the forest. One day…

◆ Plants help us by…

◆ The best part about climbing a tree…

◆ If I had a garden…

◆ I found the strangest animal living in the tree…

Barn

Follow these steps to draw.

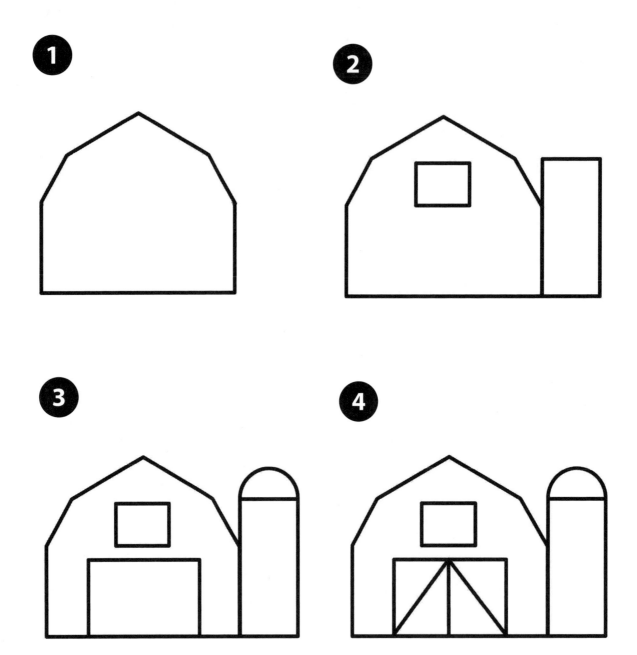

Cabin

Follow these steps to draw.

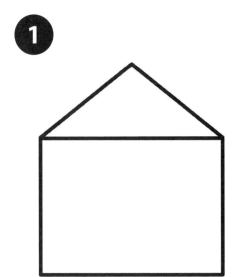

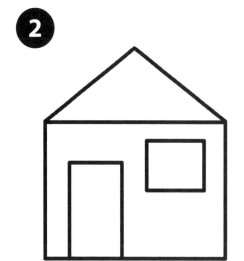

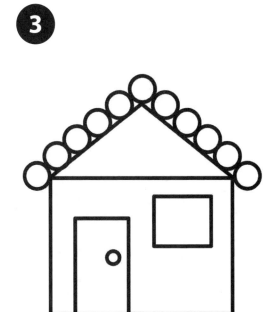

Castle

Follow these steps to draw.

 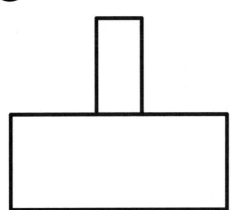

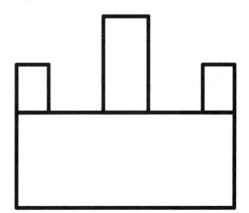

House

Follow these steps to draw.

1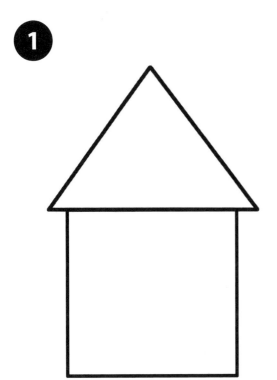

2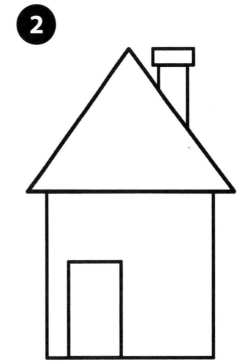

3

4

Lighthouse

Follow these steps to draw.

1

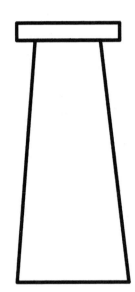

2

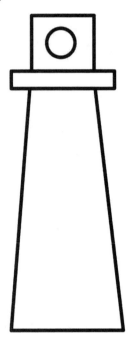

3

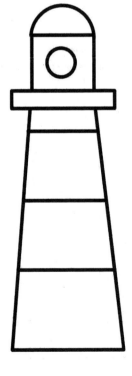

4

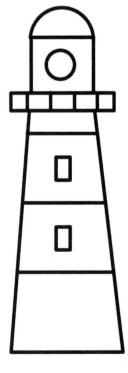

Skyscraper

Follow these steps to draw.

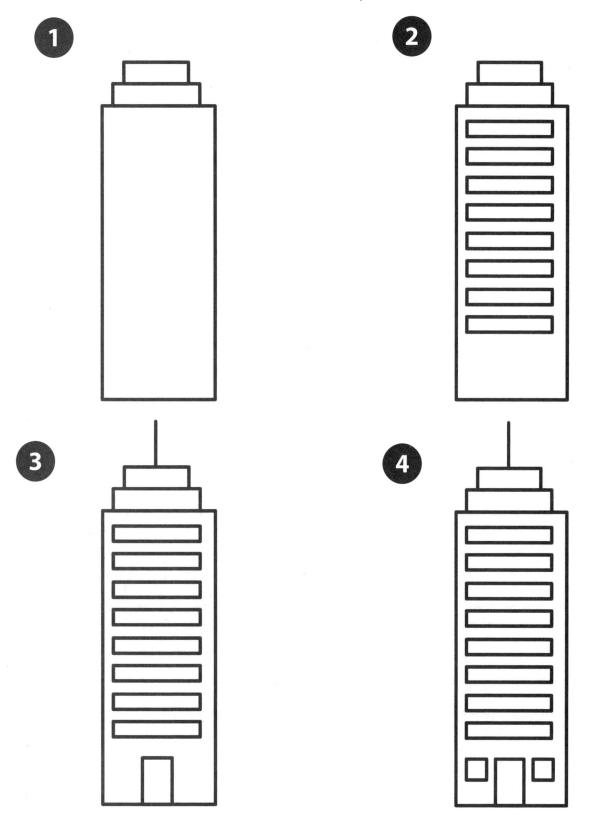

Store

Follow these steps to draw.

1

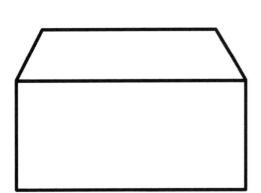

2

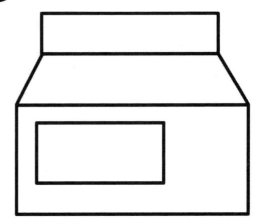

3

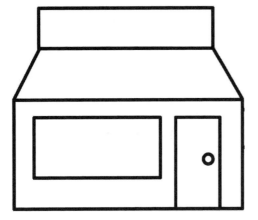

4

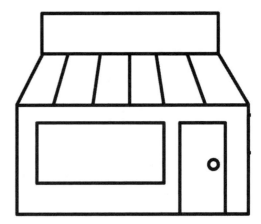

Structures Writing Prompts

◆ The barn doors opened as the sun rose. All the animals on the farm were excited because…

◆ The old barn needed a new coat of paint. The farmer decided to get the animals to help…

◆ Visiting the cabin by the lake was lots of fun.

◆ It was a cold winter night in the cabin. The fire was lit and dinner was cooking.

◆ If I lived in a castle…

◆ The castle was big and tall. Inside there were many magical secrets.

◆ The house had three front windows and a big blue door. As I walked up to the door…

◆ It was the spookiest house on the street.

◆ This was a very special house made out of…

◆ The lighthouse stood at the edge of the water. It was flashing its light to…

◆ I looked up at the skyscraper. I wondered if…

◆ Living in a skyscraper was…

◆ This was the best store ever!

◆ This was not just any store. This store sold…

◆ I was walking by the…

◆ Home sweet home…

◆ This place reminds me of…

Hot Air Balloon

Follow these steps to draw.

1

2

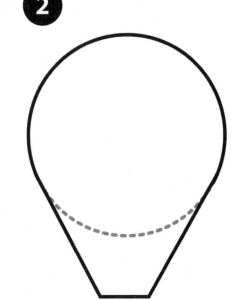

3

4

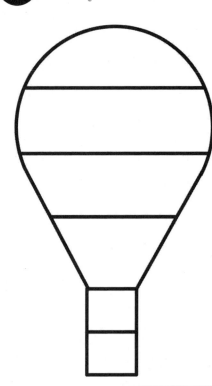

© Chalkboard Publishing

Use an eraser to remove overlapping lines.

Airplane

Follow these steps to draw.

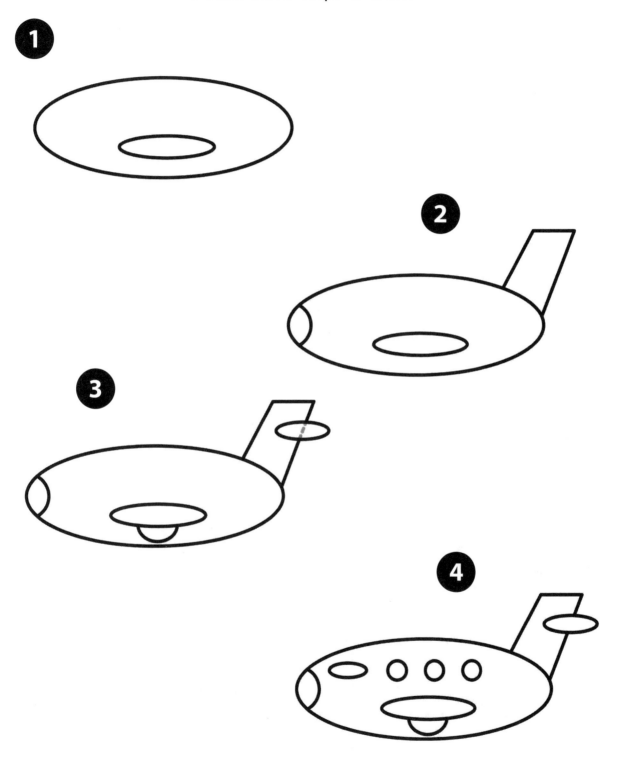

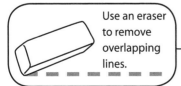

Rocket

Follow these steps to draw.

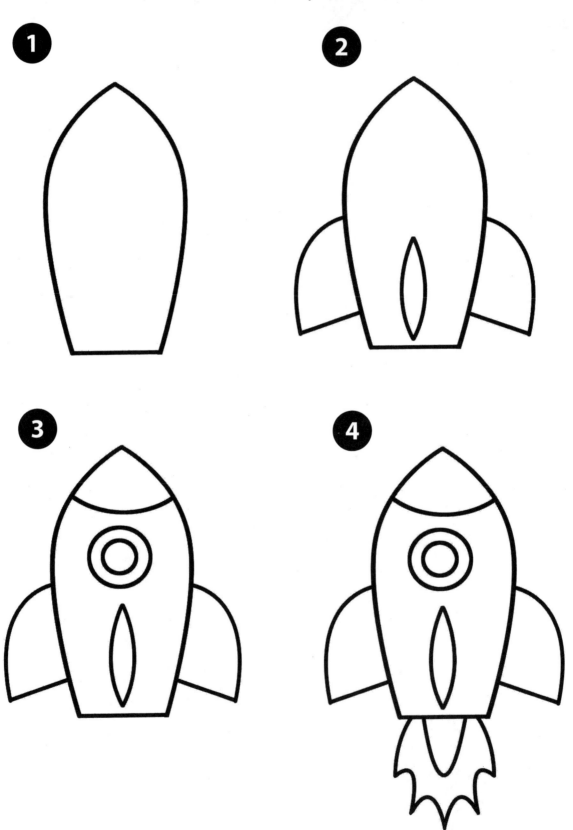

Sailboat

Follow these steps to draw.

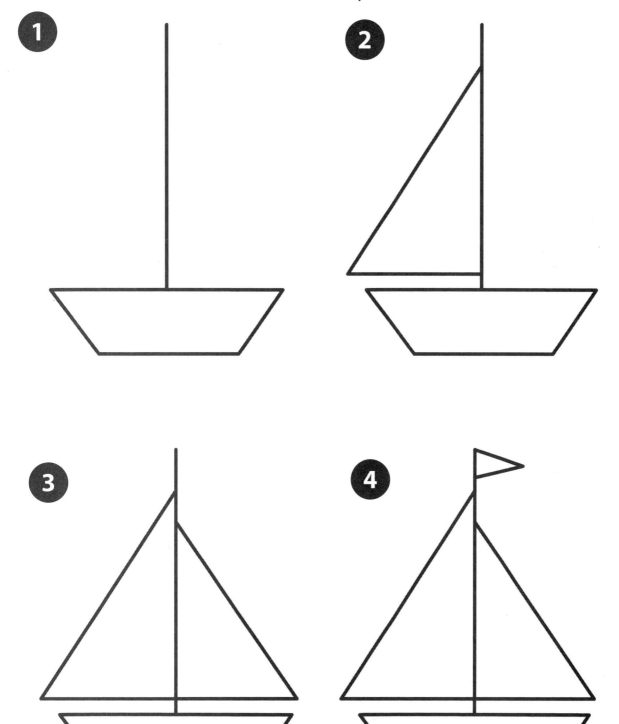

Cruise Ship

Follow these steps to draw.

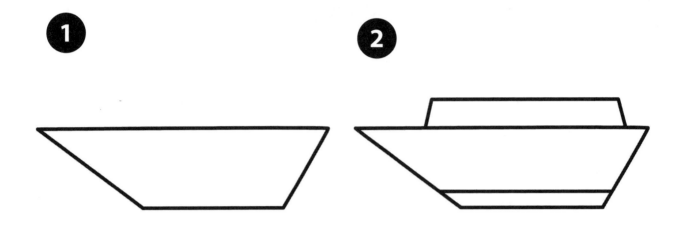

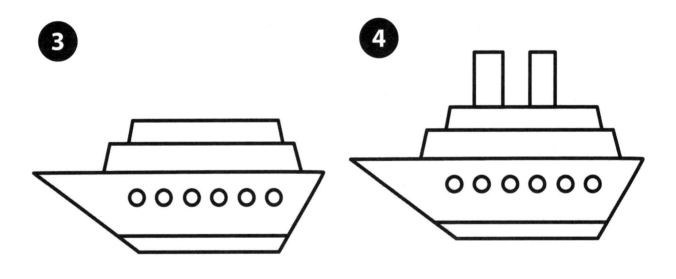

Car

Follow these steps to draw.

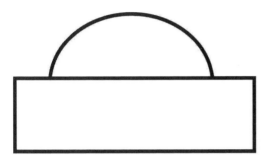

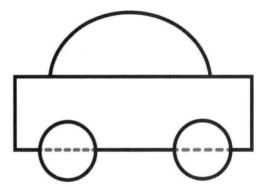

Use an eraser to remove overlapping lines.

Modern Train

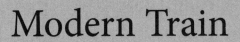

Follow these steps to draw.

1

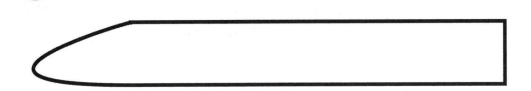

2

3

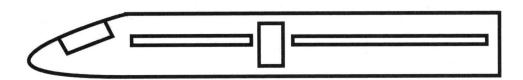

4

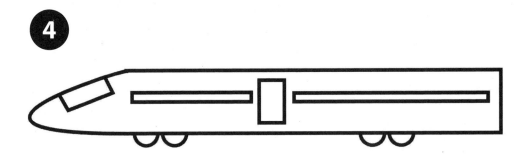

Old Train

Follow these steps to draw.

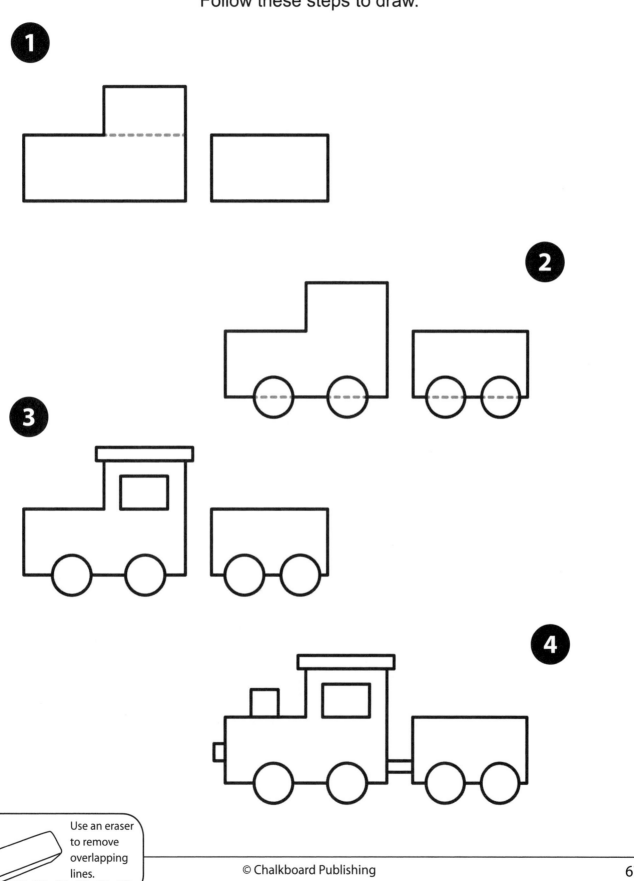

Use an eraser to remove overlapping lines.

Skateboard

Follow these steps to draw.

1

2

3

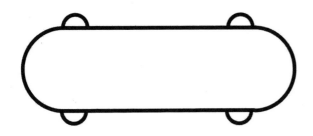

4

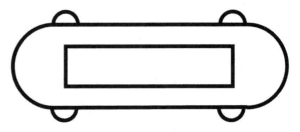

Use an eraser to remove overlapping lines.

Transportation Writing Prompts

◆ As the airplane flew over the mountain…

◆ I had never been on a _____ before.

◆ There was a mysterious car parked on the street.

◆ It would be fun to ride on a _____.

◆ One night, as the ship sailed on the ocean…

◆ The hot air balloon went up, up, and…

◆ When the children went for a hot air balloon ride, they felt like…

◆ The electric train travelled quickly through the tunnel. On the other side, there was a…

◆ Electric trains travel very fast.

◆ The steam engine travelled toward the station, when all of a sudden..

◆ The steam engine was really a time machine.

◆ The astronauts got into the rocket. They were going to…

◆ The rocketship blasted off into space. It was off to the planet…

◆ It was a perfect day for sailing.

◆ _____ went for a fantastic skateboard ride.

◆ I designed a super car. My car can…

◆ One morning, I woke up and saw a rocketship in my backyard.

◆ So I decided to build a rocketship…

◆ It was noisy and bumpy ride.

◆ My trip in a…

More Writing Ideas

Story-Writing Workshop

Have students write a story using the Story Writing Workshop template (pages 75–78) as an outline to guide their writing. When students are finished, provide them with choices such as using computer programs to design, illustrate, print, and publish their story.

Acrostic Poems

Describe to students the conventions of an acrostic poem. A name or word is written vertically, with one letter on each line. Each letter is then used to start a short sentence or a word that describes, or is related in some way to, the original name or word. For example,

S　is for my sister Sara

A　is for always laughing with me

R　is for her red, wavy hair

A　is for the art she draws so well

Cinquain Poem

A cinquain poem has five lines and describes a person, place, or thing. The poem has a pattern, but does not have to rhyme. Show students examples of cinquains to help them become familiar with the form.

Dog	a one-word title, a noun
brown, furry	two adjectives
barking, running, jumping	three *-ing* participles
having fun	phrase
pet	a synonym for your title, another noun

Greeting Card

Brainstorm with students a list of reasons why people give greeting cards. Then have students decide on a message for their card and create it. Use the how-to-draw pages in this book as inspiration. Encourage students to convey their message through a riddle, poetry, or the use of humor.

Design a Poster

Posters advertise many things, such as events, concerts, CDs, movies, television shows, clothing, products, places, stores, vehicles, and vacation destinations. They also advertise upcoming events. Have students create a poster to advertise something from the above list, or of their own choosing, using the how-to-draw pages from this book as inspiration. Remind them to use persuasive words and phrases.

Special Stamp

Use the Amazing Stamp template (page 82) so students can create their own personal stamp. Brainstorm people and things they have seen on stamps. Ask students why these people and things might have been presented in that form. Recall with students that subjects on stamps include provincial plants and animals, endangered species, and important places. Then have students create their own stamp to send out a message about what is important to them.

Person, Place, or Thing Collage

Have students choose a person, place, or thing to draw. Have students draw the picture on a large piece of paper. Then have students write descriptive words or phrases around the picture.

Personal Postcard

Have students use the Personal Postcard template (page 87) to create postcards from real or imaginary places.

Wanted Poster

Have students create a wanted poster (page 86) inspired by a how-to-draw page from this book. Use the Wanted Poster template as a base to create a poster. Encourage them to use attention-grabbing words, such as *fastest, slowest, strongest, meanest, craziest,* or *loudest,* to describe the character and why they are wanted. Remind them to include a reward for capture. Students could also include where the character was last seen.

Draw a Map

Maps serve many purposes. Maps can show the location of towns, cities, states, countries, and continents. Maps can also show the location of places inside buildings, malls, zoos, and amusement parks. Have students use My Marvelous Map template (page 89) to draw a map showing the places in an imaginary city, zoo, or any place they choose. Maps can be simple or detailed, according to students' abilities. Remind students to include a legend. Have students write about their map describing each of the places marked on it.

More Writing Prompts

1. Would you rather sound like a _____ or a _____? Explain.

2. Would you rather have the abilities of a _____ or a _____? Explain.

3. Would you rather look like a _____ or a _____? Explain.

4. Would you rather live in a _____ or a _____? Explain.

5. Would you rather have a _____ or a _____ for a pet? Explain.

6. Would you rather go visit a _____ or a _____? Expain.

7. Would you rather be a _____ or a _____? Explain.

8. Would you rather travel by _____ or a _____? Explain.

9. Would you rather have a _____ or _____ for a babysitter for a day? Explain.

10. Would you rather take a _____ or a _____ to school for a day? Explain.

Adjectives for Writing

Category	Adjectives
Size	big, small, short, tall, fat, skinny, large, medium, slim, thin, slender, tiny, lean, scrawny, huge, gigantic, jumbo, plump, wee, wide, narrow, colossal, mountainous
Shape	round, square, pointed, jagged, oval, chunky, curly, straight, curved, flat, twisted, heart-shaped, spiky, crooked, wavy, bent, gnarled, tangled, messy
Color	red, orange, yellow, green, blue, purple, pink, gray, white, black, brown, silver, gold
Age	young, old, ancient, youthful, aged, new, baby, newborn
Sound	loud, quite, long, short, musical, irritating, enjoyable, surprising, soft, noisy, thunderous, blaring, muffled, whispering, growling, grumbling
Light and Brightness	dull, bright, dark, light, clear, brilliant, flashy, flashing, dim, faint, glowing, flickering, twinkly, twinkling, shiny, shining
Smell	good, bad, strong, sweet, salty, spicy, stinky, sour, delicious, yummy, fresh, rotten, rotting
Feel and Texture	soft, hard, smooth, rough, silky, fluffy, fuzzy, furry, wet, dry, bumpy, lumpy, scratchy, sweaty, slippery, slimy, gritty, dirty, sticky, gummy, jiggly, wiggly, squishy, watery, liquid, solid, rock hard, damp, stiff, firm, comfortable, uncomfortable
Taste	delicious, bitter, sweet, salty, tasty, spicy, yummy, bland, sour, strong
Speed and Movement	quick, quickly, fast, slow, slowly, rapid, rapidly, sluggish, sluggishly, brisk, briskly, swift, swiftly, prompt, promptly, instant, instantly, immediate, immediately, late, lately
Temperature	hot, cold, icy, frosty, chilly, burning, boiling, steamy, sizzling, cool, warm, frigid, freezing, frozen, damp, humid, melting, comfortable, uncomfortable

Story-Writing Workshop

Story Title: _____

Beginning

☐ I wrote an attention-grabbing first sentence.

☐ I introduced the main character.

☐ I wrote about where the story takes place.

_____

_____

_____

_____

_____

_____

_____

_____

_____

_____

☐ I checked the spelling and punctuation. ☐ I added adjectives.

Middle ☐ **I explained the problem in the story.**

_____

_____

_____

_____

_____

_____

_____

_____

_____

_____

_____

_____

_____

☐ **I checked the spelling and punctuation.** ☐ **I added adjectives.**

Events | ☐ **I wrote about events that happen in the story before the problem is solved.**

Event 1: _____

_____

_____

_____

_____

_____

Event 2: _____

_____

_____

_____

_____

_____

☐ **I checked the spelling and punctuation.**   ☐ **I added adjectives.**

Ending ☐ I explained how the problem was solved.

_____

_____

_____

_____

_____

_____

_____

_____

_____

_____

_____

_____

_____

_____

☐ I checked the spelling and punctuation. ☐ I added adjectives.

Super Story

Story Title: _____

BEGINNING:

_____

_____

_____

_____

_____

_____

[ ] **I checked the spelling and punctuation.** [ ] **I added adjectives.**

MIDDLE:

_____

_____

_____

_____

_____

_____

_____

☐ I checked the spelling and punctuation. ☐ I added adjectives.

ENDING:

_____

_____

_____

_____

_____

_____

_____

_____

☐ **I checked the spelling and punctuation.** ☐ **I added adjectives.**

Amazing Stamp

Draw and color an amazing stamp.

Write about your stamp. _____

_____

_____

Acrostic Poem

Acrostic poems are poems in which the first letter of each line forms a word or phrase (vertically). An acrostic poem can describe the subject or even tell a brief story about it.

Cinquain Poem

Cinquains (sing-cane) are just five lines long, with only a few words on each line. Cinquain poems are often diamond shaped.

Write a five-line cinquain poem.

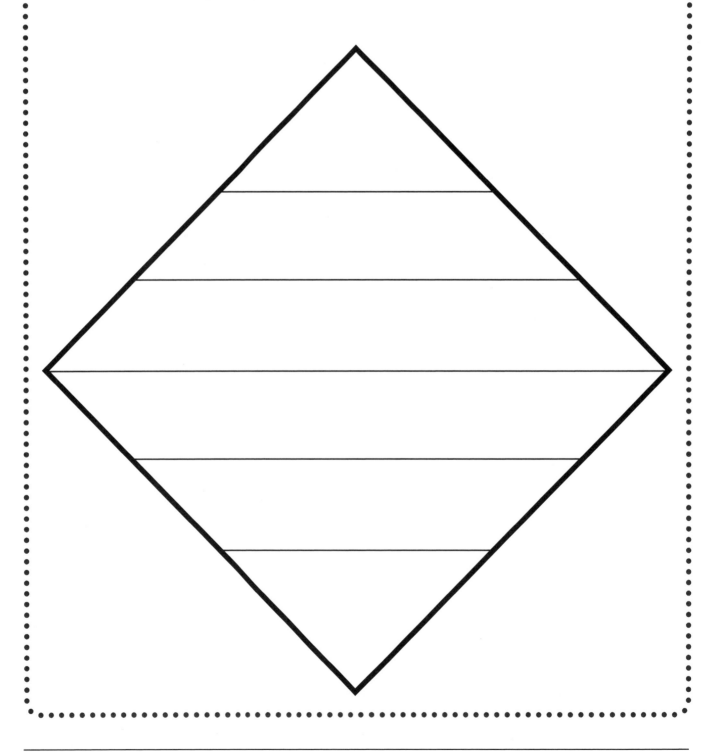

Animal Report

My pet is a/an : _____

Name of my pet : _____

My pet is a/an :   mammal   reptile   amphibian   fish   bird

Does the animal breathe air?	
What is the animal's habitat?	
What does the animal eat?	
What special characteristics does the animal have?	
Interesting fact	
Interesting fact	
Interesting fact	

WANTED!

Name:

_____

Last seen:

_____

_____

Description:

_____

_____

Wanted for:

_____

_____

Reward:

_____

Personal Postcard

Write a postcard to a friend.

Front of Postcard:

Back of Postcard:

To:

News Story

Use this planner to write a news story.

Headline _____

Who is the story about?

_____

What happened?

_____

_____

_____

_____

_____

_____

Where did the story happen?

_____

_____

_____

When did the story happen?

_____

_____

My Marvelous Map

A map is a flat drawing of a place. Choose a place and draw a map. Create a legend that includes symbols to help people find things on your map.

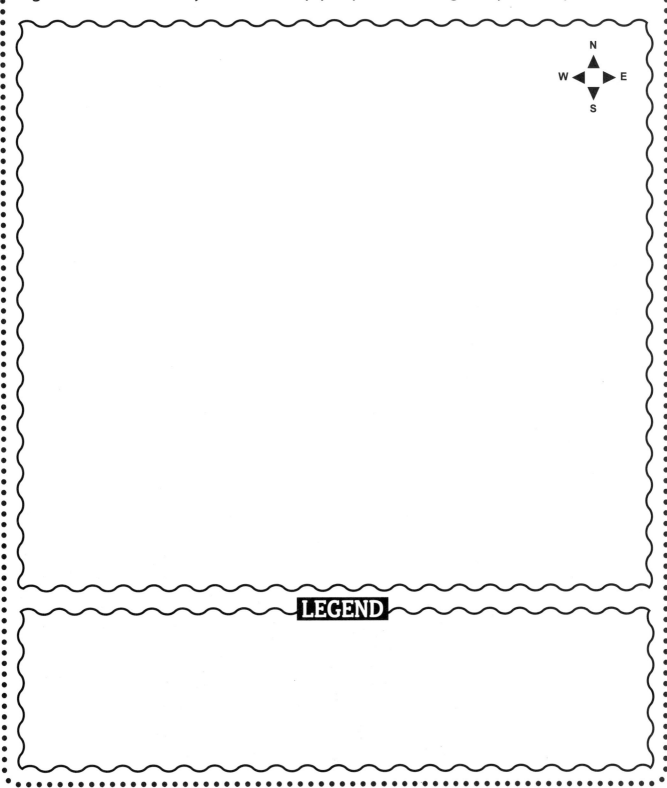

LEGEND

Journal Page

Subject : _____

[ ] **I checked the spelling and punctuation.**

Story Title _____

One day,

_____

_____

_____

_____

First,

_____

_____

_____

Next,

_____

_____

_____

Then,

_____

_____

_____

After that,

_____

_____

_____

Finally,

_____

_____

_____

Web of Ideas

Subject : _____

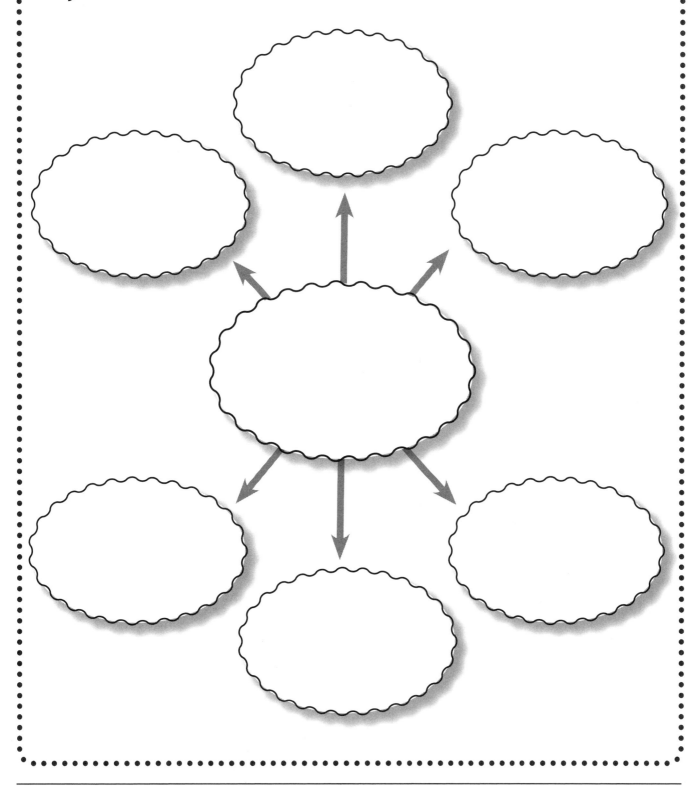

Comparison Chart

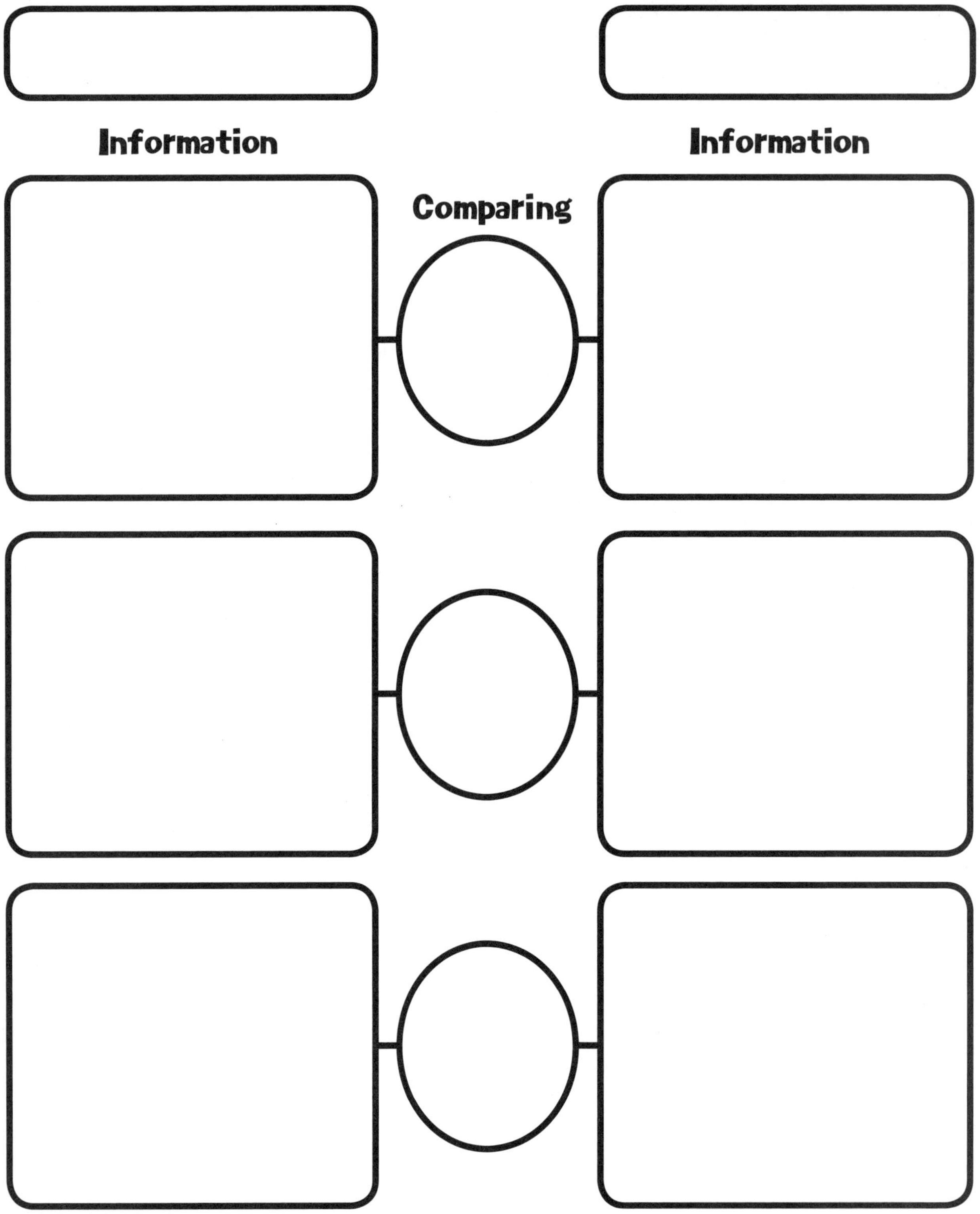

Information

Information

Comparing

How Am I Doing?

	Completing my work	Using my time wisely	Following directions	Keeping organized
Full speed ahead!	• My work is always complete and done with care. • I added extra details to my work.	• I always get my work done on time.	• I always follow directions.	• My materials are always neatly organized. • I am always prepared and ready to learn.
Keep going!	• My work is complete and done with care. • I added extra details to my work.	• I usually get my work done on time.	• I usually follow directions without reminders.	• I usually can find my materials. • I am usually prepared and ready to learn.
Slow down!	• My work is complete. • I need to check my work.	• I sometimes get my work done on time.	• I sometimes need reminders to follow directions.	• I sometimes need time to find my materials. • I am sometimes prepared and ready to learn.
Stop!	• My work is not complete. • I need to check my work.	• I rarely get my work done on time.	• I need reminders to follow directions.	• I need to organize my materials. • I am rarely prepared and ready to learn.

CONGRATULATIONS !

_____

YOU CAN DRAW AND WRITE!